W9-CNQ-225

★ IT'S MY STATE! ★

ARIZONA

Kathleen Derzipilski

Amanda Hudson

Marshall Cavendish
Benchmark
New York

Website: www.marshallcavendish.us

This publication represents the opinions and views of the authors based on their personal experience, knowledge, and research. The information in this book serves as a general guide only. The authors and publisher have used their best efforts in preparing this book and disclaim liability rising directly and indirectly from the use and application of this book.

Other Marshall Cavendish Offices:
Marshall Cavendish International (Asia) Private Limited, 1 New Industrial Road, Singapore 536196 •
Marshall Cavendish International (Thailand) Co Ltd. 253 Asoke, 12th Flr, Sukhumvit 21 Road, Klongtoey Nua, Wattana, Bangkok 10110, Thailand • Marshall Cavendish (Malaysia) Sdn Bhd, Times Subang, Lot 46, Subang Hi-Tech Industrial Park, Batu Tiga, 40000 Shah Alam, Selangor Darul Ehsan, Malaysia

Marshall Cavendish is a trademark of Times Publishing Limited

All websites were available and accurate when this book was sent to press.

Library of Congress Cataloging-in-Publication Data
Derzipilski, Kathleen.
        Arizona / Kathleen Derzipilski and Amanda Hudson.—2nd ed.
            p. cm. — (It's my state!)
        Includes bibliographical references and index.
        ISBN 978-1-60870-521-4 (print) — ISBN 978-1-60870-699-0 (ebook)
        1. Arizona—Juvenile literature. I. Hudson, Amanda, 1977- II. Title.
    F811.3.D47 2012
    979.1—dc22   2010044330

Second Edition developed for Marshall Cavendish Benchmark by RJF Publishing LLC (www.RJFpublishing.com)
Series Designer, Second Edition: Tammy West/Westgraphix LLC
Editor, Second Edition: Emily Dolbear

All maps, illustrations, and graphics © Marshall Cavendish Corporation. Maps and artwork on pages 6, 42, 43, 75, 76, and back cover by Christopher Santoro. Map and graphics on pages 8 and 40 by Westgraphix LLC.

The photographs in this book are used by permission and through the courtesy of:
Front cover: SDM IMAGES/Alamy and Seth Joel/Getty (inset).
Alamy: George H.H. Huey, 4 (left), 24; Juniors Bildarchiv, 4 (right); Gaertner, 5 (left); Rick and Nora Bowers, 5 (right), 21 (right); Michael Runkel Arizona, 9; Tom Bean, 10, 14; Don Kates, 11; Buddy Mays, 12; Kevin Schafer, 13; Kevin Ebi, 16; David Watts, 17; Bob Gibbons, 19; Mira, 20; Genevieve Vallee, 21 (left); Skip Higgins of Raskal Photography, 22; Dennis MacDonald, 27; North Wind Picture Archives, 28; Pictorial Press Ltd, 30; David South, 35; rshantz, 36; Hemis, 38; R1, 39; Tomas Abad, 45; Allstar Picture Library, 49 (left); Norma Jean Gargasz, 50, 53 (top); Matthew Heinrichs, 54; Robert Harding Picture Library, Ltd, 58; rabh images, 60; Jim West, 62, 64; Caro, 65; Susan E. Degginger, 66, 67, 72; Leslie Garland Picture Library, 70; Bill Bachmann, 71 (right); Transtock Inc., 71 (left); Ron Niebrugge, 74. **Associated Press:** Associated Press, 47. **Corbis:** Bettman, 26. **Getty Images:** Getty Images, 31, 32, 46, 49 (right), 57, 69; Roll Call, 41; Sony BMG Music Entertainment, 48; Panoramic Images, 53 (bottom). **The Image Works:** Jack Kurtz, 52. **National Geographic Stock:** Joel Sartore, 18. **Superstock:** Richard Cummins, 51.

Printed in Malaysia (T).
135642

ARIZONA

CONTENTS

A Quick Look at
ARIZONA

State Flower: Saguaro Cactus Blossom

Saguaro blossoms grow on the tips of the arms of the saguaro cactus. The cactus, which grows only in the Sonoran Desert, blooms every year from mid-May to mid-June. The white blossoms have a very short life. They typically open at night and close the next day. Some of the flowers develop into sweet, juicy fruits full of tiny seeds.

State Tree: Palo Verde

Palo verde is Spanish for "green stick." The tree gets its name from the green bark on its branches and trunk. In the spring, fragrant yellow flowers cover the trees. Palo verde seeds are very hard, but creatures such as rock squirrels rely on the seeds for food. The trees grow in sandy areas and rocky hillsides throughout the Sonoran Desert.

State Bird: Cactus Wren

The cactus wren, chosen as the state bird by the Arizona state legislature in 1931, is the largest wren in North America. Cactus wrens are insect eaters. They like to build their large, round nests inside cholla or other cactus plants. The prickly cactus spines provide protection for the nest, which is lined with soft feathers.

State Neckwear: Bolo Tie

The bolo tie was adopted as Arizona's official state neckwear in 1973. A silversmith from Wickenberg named Victor Cedarstaff claims to have invented the tie in the 1940s. The bolo tie is a long leather cord that tightens around the neck with a sliding clasp. The clasp is often made of beautiful silver with polished minerals and stones.

State Gem: Turquoise

Turquoise is a blue-green gemstone that contains copper and aluminum. Many American Indian groups of the Southwest use the gemstone in jewelry, crafts, and ceremonies. Long ago, the native people of Arizona and New Mexico mined turquoise and carried the valued gem along the trade routes to Mexico.

State Amphibian: Arizona Tree Frog

In 1986, the Arizona tree frog was officially named the state amphibian, after Arizona schoolchildren voted for it in a poll. The small frog is green and brown and lives mainly in the oak, pine, and fir forests of central Arizona's mountains. Arizona tree frogs can measure from ¾ inch (2 centimeters) to 2 inches (5 cm) long. The pads on their toes allow the tree frogs to climb tall trees. They have been found as high as 75 feet (23 meters).

ARIZONA

Grand Canyon

Lake Powell

Monument Valley

Kayenta

Lake Mead

Humphreys Peak

Window Rock

Colorado River

Flagstaff

Prescott

Payson

Tonto River

Theodore Roosevelt Lake

Salt River

Phoenix

Gila River

Tempe

Mt. Lemmon

Gila River

Yuma

Tucson

San Xavier del Bac Mission

N

W   E

S

MEXICO

The Grand Canyon State

Arizona is a large state located in the southwestern United States. It is the sixth-largest U.S. state, measuring 113,635 square miles (294,313 square kilometers) in land area. It has fifteen counties. The state is shaped almost like a square and measures approximately 400 miles (645 km) from north to south and 310 miles (500 km) from west to east. Arizona received its nickname, the Grand Canyon State, from the famous landform in the northwestern part of the state.

Arizona's landscape is commonly divided into three geographical regions: the Colorado Plateau in the north, the Arizona transition zone in the middle, and the Basin and Range region in the south. Generally, the state's higher elevations, ranging from 5,000 to 8,000 feet (1,525 to 2,440 m), are in the north.

The Colorado Plateau

The Colorado Plateau is a traditional western landscape made up of plateaus, small plateaus called mesas, and even smaller plateaus called buttes. It is covered by ancient lava flows and cut by canyons. The canyons and buttes reveal layers of stone, minerals, ash, and fossils. The region's rivers helped create the

Quick Facts

ARIZONA BORDERS

North	Utah
South	Mexico
East	Colorado
	New Mexico
West	California
	Nevada

Arizona Counties

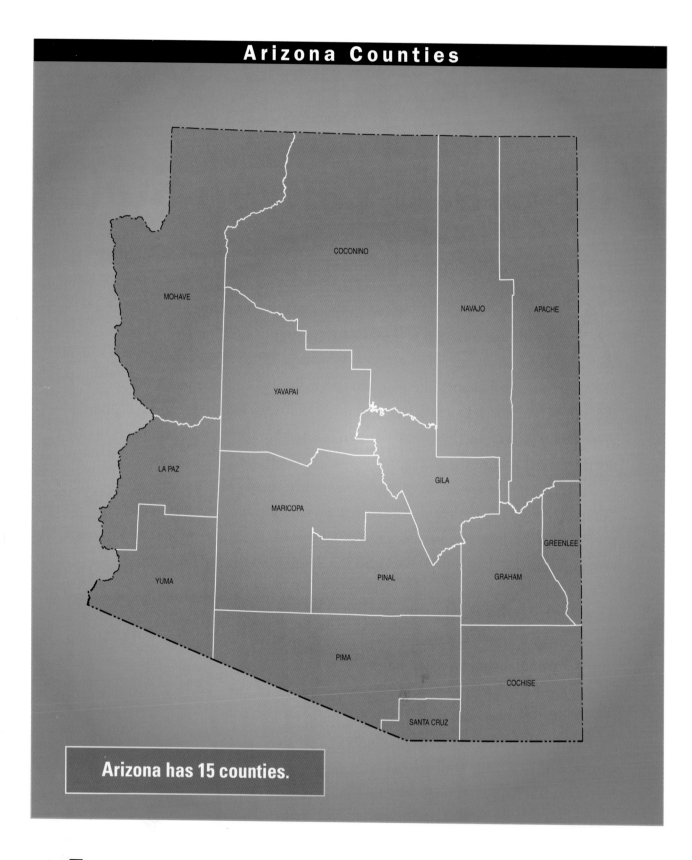

Arizona has 15 counties.

canyons as they wore down the rocks over millions of years.

Located in the western part of the Colorado Plateau is the most famous of Arizona's canyons—the Grand Canyon, a popular vacation destination for people from all over the world. The average depth of the canyon is about 1 mile (1.6 km), with the Colorado River flowing 5,000 feet (1,525 m) below the canyon's rim. Rainwater and snowmelt helped the Colorado River form the Grand Canyon, which is 18 miles (29 km) across at its widest point. The canyon is 277 miles (446 km) long and splinters into many side canyons. Although the world has larger and deeper canyons, the Grand Canyon is considered one of the most beautiful. U.S. geologist John Wesley Powell explored the Grand Canyon and the Colorado River in 1869. He wrote about the immensity and grandeur of the canyon, describing it as "a broad, deep, flaring gorge of many colors." Scientists estimate that the oldest rocks in the canyon are close to 2 billion years old.

In Their Own Words

The spectacle is so symmetrical, and so completely excludes the outside world and its accustomed standards, it is with difficulty one can acquire any notion of its immensity.

—Author C. A. Higgins, on the Grand Canyon

The Grand Canyon is Arizona's most popular tourist attraction. Nearly 5 million people visit the canyon each year.

The San Francisco Volcanic Field is filled with dormant or extinct volcanoes.

North of the Grand Canyon is an area called the Kaibab Plateau. The plateau is heavily forested with aspen, spruce, fir, and ponderosa pine.

South of the Grand Canyon, along the southern edge of the Colorado Plateau, is an area of 1,800 square miles (4,660 sq km) filled with hundreds of dormant or extinct volcanoes. (Dormant volcanoes are not currently erupting, though it is possible they may erupt in the future. Extinct volcanoes are not currently erupting and are not expected to erupt in the future.) This area, known as the San Francisco Volcanic Field, creates a scenic background for the city of Flagstaff. Most of the hills and mountains found between Flagstaff and the Grand Canyon are actually extinct volcanoes. The highest of these peaks is Humphreys Peak. It rises 12,633 feet (3,851 m) and is the highest point in Arizona. The state's youngest volcano, Sunset Crater, erupted sometime between 1040 and 1100 CE. It has been a national monument since 1930.

Erosion—the wearing away of land by wind and water over time—has shaped the eastern part of the Colorado Plateau. The strange shapes and rock formations of the badlands and the Painted Desert were carved by erosion. The wearing away of the land has also uncovered the mineral-filled logs of the Petrified Forest. In this forest, the wood petrified, or slowly changed into rocklike, mineral-rich material. The isolated buttes and mesas of Monument Valley in northeastern Arizona were also formed by erosion. The steep cliffs of the Mogollon Rim mark the southern boundary of the Colorado Plateau.

Arizona Transition Zone

Numerous mountain ranges fill the Arizona transition zone, located in a narrow strip of land across the middle of the state. The region is a transitional area between the higher elevations of the Colorado Plateau and the lower Basin and Range region. The area, sometimes called the "copper belt," is rich with deposits of copper-bearing minerals. The highest mountains in the transition zone are forested with Douglas fir and ponderosa pine trees. Pinyon pine and juniper grow at the lower elevations.

The Painted Desert is named for its colorful rock formations.

Phoenix is the capital of Arizona and the state's largest city.

Arizona's largest city, Phoenix, is located in the center of the state. Many people come to central Arizona to visit this city. People also come to fish in the shady streams of the transition zone. During the winter months, many people ski and snowboard here. Loggers harvest the forests of the White Mountains in eastern Arizona. The state's second-highest mountain, Baldy Peak, is in the White Mountains. This peak, sometimes called Mount Baldy by Arizonans, rises to 11,420 feet (3,480 m).

In Their Own Words

There is no shortage of water in the desert but exactly the right amount, a perfect ratio of water to rock, of water to sand, insuring that wide, free, open, generous spacing among plants and animals, homes and towns and cities.

—Environmentalist Edward Abbey, from his book *Desert Solitaire* (1968)

Basin and Range

The Basin and Range region extends over southern Arizona. It is an expansive flat land with basins that are interrupted by abrupt, jagged mountains. The basins are shallow valleys that look like big, dry ponds. The effects of erosion mark this region too. The wind continues to carry away the soil and the fine sand from the dry, hard ground. The city of Tucson is located here, in the southern third of Arizona.

The massive Sonoran Desert occupies the southwestern part of Arizona. This desert has a total area of 120,000 square miles (311,000 sq km) and extends west into California and south into Mexico. The Sonoran Desert is one of the hottest and driest deserts in North America. The hottest and driest sections surround the Colorado River. The tall, upright saguaro cactus, a common symbol for the state of Arizona, grows only in the Sonoran Desert. The desert is also home to small trees such as mesquite and ironwood, which give some shade to the area. The creosote bush is the most common shrub in the driest lower elevations.

The saguaro cactus is found only in the Sonoran Desert.

Sprawling prickly pear, cholla cactus, and compact barrel cactus grow here too. Living among these plants are scorpions, reptiles such as rattlesnakes and Gila monsters, and various birds.

Besides the Sonoran, Arizona also has parts of three other major deserts. The Mojave is located in the northwestern part of the state. Northeastern Arizona

The Little Colorado River is a tributary of the Colorado River.

is home to the Great Basin Desert, and the Chihuahuan Desert is located in the state's southeastern corner.

Rivers

The waters of nearly all the rivers in Arizona eventually flow into the Colorado River. Among its tributaries, or smaller rivers that are connected to it, are the Little Colorado, the Bill Williams, and the Gila rivers. The Gila is the second major river of Arizona, after the Colorado. It flows east to west across southern Arizona. The Salt River and the San Pedro River are tributaries of the Gila.

Dams across Arizona's major rivers form reservoirs and other artificial lakes. Water stored behind the dams is used to irrigate crops and to supply the needs of people living in urban areas. Hydroelectric plants at these dams generate electricity using the power of the flowing water. The Hoover Dam, on the Arizona-Nevada border, was constructed on the Colorado River in the 1930s. It formed Lake Mead (located partly in Arizona and partly in Nevada), one of the largest artificial lakes in the world. The Theodore Roosevelt Dam was completed in 1911. This dam, built across the Salt River in south-central Arizona, helped to make Arizona an important agricultural region.

Climate

The wide range of landforms and elevations in Arizona creates extremes in the state's weather and climate. The southwestern corner of the state receives only 3 to 4 inches (8 to 10 cm) of rain a year—the least amount in the state. The state averages about 10 to 20 inches (25 to 50 cm) of precipitation each year. Many people think of Arizona as a desert, but the high mountains and Colorado

The Twin Buttes can be seen near Sedona. This region receives frequent thunderstorms in the summer.

Plateau can receive 10 feet (3 m) or more of snow every year. The melting of this snow helps to supply the state's main rivers. Arizona has two rainy seasons. Gentle rains fall during the winter, between December and March. Arizona receives most of its annual rainfall during the summer monsoon season, between July and September. During this time, summer storms can be quick and severe. A thunderstorm can pass through an area, hitting it with hailstones, sharp winds, and lightning. Rushing water soon floods the narrow canyons and the streets.

Arizona also has a cycle of wet years followed by years of drought. During a drought, some areas receive no rainfall at all. Farmland dries out and cannot produce enough crops. Livestock and other animals also suffer from the lack of water. During times of drought, the danger of forest fires increases because the plants and trees are so dry.

Temperatures in the state also vary. Daytime temperatures in July can top 110 degrees Fahrenheit (43 degrees Celsius) in southern Arizona. The state's high plateaus average a more comfortable 90 °F (32 °C). In January, the temperature averages above 50 °F (10 °C) in southern Arizona. In the northern parts of the state and in the high mountains, temperatures can drop to below freezing after the sun goes down.

Wildlife

Some animals, such as coyotes, cottontails, bats, bobcats, squirrels, skunks, raccoons, foxes, and mule deer, live throughout Arizona. Small herds of antelope graze on the grasslands in the northern and southern parts of the state. Black bears, the only species of bear in Arizona, live in woodland areas. Javelina, or peccary, look like small wild pigs and roam among the cactus and mesquite. Mud turtles live in the ponds and rivers of the south-central part of the state.

In the desert, tortoises protect themselves from heat and cold by burrowing in the sand. Numerous snakes and lizards bask on the rocks or wait in the shade. The Gila monster, a large venomous lizard, lives in the desert.

A great variety of migrating birds stop in the Chiricahua Mountains of southeastern Arizona. Arizona is also known for its beautiful butterflies.

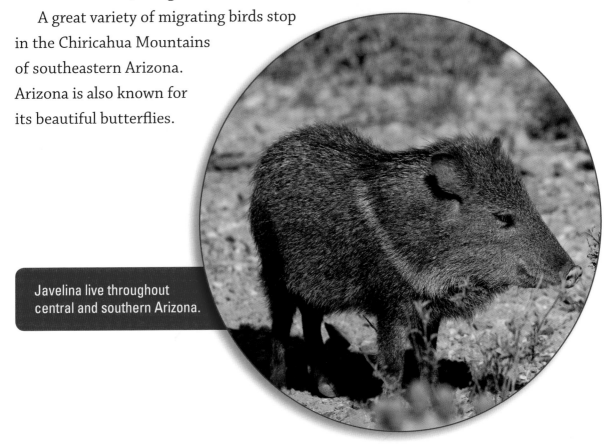

Javelina live throughout central and southern Arizona.

Endangered Species in Arizona

Loss of or changes in natural habitats can cause animal and plant species to become endangered—that is, so reduced in numbers that they are at risk of becoming extinct, or completely dying out. The building of cities and towns and the polluting of land and water most often affect natural habitats. The animals may not be able to find food or safe places to live. The plants may not thrive any longer. Some of Arizona's wildlife is in danger of disappearing, but many organizations and concerned residents are working together to try to help some of these endangered species.

The razorback sucker, or the humpback sucker, is a fish native to Arizona. It lives on the sandy bottom of rivers with strong currents. To spawn, or breed, it seeks quieter wetlands and backwaters. These fish used to live throughout the basins of the Gila and the Colorado rivers. Today, only a few hundred razorback suckers remain in the wild. The largest surviving population is found in Lake Mohave, behind Davis Dam on the Colorado River. Dams have changed the river currents and the sediments on the riverbeds. Dams also act as barriers and can prevent the razorbacks from migrating to their spawning areas.

To increase the number of razorback suckers, people are raising the fish in hatcheries. When the hatchery fish are old enough, they are released into the wild to live and breed with wild fish. Scientists are hopeful that the razorback sucker will survive. Although more than 12 million razorbacks have been released into the Colorado River basin, most have been eaten by nonnative fish.

A subspecies of gray wolf called the Mexican gray wolf is also endangered in Arizona. The wolves were

The razorback sucker
is an endangered species.

Environmental groups have worked to increase the Mexican gray wolf population in Arizona.

once common in central Arizona. By the 1900s, they threatened livestock in the area, and efforts to control the wolves drastically reduced their numbers. By the 1970s, the Mexican gray wolf had almost disappeared from the United States and Mexico. The U.S. Fish and Wildlife Service listed this animal as an endangered species in 1976.

U.S. and Mexican wildlife agencies agreed to work together on a captive breeding program. In 1998, eleven wolves that had been raised in captivity were released into the Blue Range Wolf Recovery Area in eastern Arizona. Additional releases have followed. In 2002, for the first time since the release program began, a wild-born litter came from a wild-born parent. By 2010, it was estimated that the wild population numbered about sixty, and approximately three hundred additional wolves were being held in captive breeding facilities.

Plants & Animals

Rattlesnake

The dull colors of rattlesnakes help them blend into their surroundings. Eleven species of rattlesnake live in Arizona. Each snake has a rattle made of dried skin at the end of its tail and hollow fangs designed for injecting venom into its prey.

Mule Deer

The mule deer gets its name from its large, mulelike ears. These deer live throughout Arizona, from the sparse deserts to the forested mountains. They feed on spring grasses, buds, bark, and twigs.

Pinyon Pine

The pinyon pine can be found in the northern forests of the high Colorado Plateau. Pinyon pines produce delicious, nutritious nuts.

Teddy Bear Cholla

The teddy bear cholla gets its name from its spines, which make it appear soft and fuzzy from a distance. Despite its cuddly appearance, this cactus is dangerous. Its fuzzy-looking spines have tiny barbs that dig under the skin, making them very difficult to remove. Teddy bear cholla grow throughout the Sonoran Desert.

White-nosed Coati

This mammal, also referred to as a coatimundi, lives in the Sonoran and Chihuahuan deserts. Similar in appearance to a raccoon, it gets its name from the white fur at the tip of its snout. Coatis eat insects, fruits, small lizards, and mice.

Black-chinned Hummingbird

The summer rainy season draws a variety of hummingbirds to Arizona. Many of them are migrating from their nesting grounds in the western United States to the tropical forests of Mexico and Central America. The black-chinned hummingbird is most common in open areas near Arizona sycamore and Fremont cottonwood trees.

From the Beginning

People have been living in what is today Arizona for at least 12,000 years. The first residents of present-day Arizona were the descendants of people who probably came to North America from Asia, crossing a land bridge that used to connect eastern Russia and Alaska. At their campsites, these early people left stone spear points called Clovis points. They hunted large grazing animals, such as mammoths and bison, which thrived on the region's grassy plains. By about 8000 BCE, the area's climate had warmed, and deserts replaced the grasslands. Most of the large animals died out.

People adjusted to these changes by hunting smaller animals, such as rabbits, and gathering nuts and berries. They eventually learned how to farm, which allowed them to settle in one place. They began to build houses of mud, stone, and wood. Many of the houses, now called pit houses, were built partially underground. Families built their houses close to each other and formed villages.

Over time, these first people developed into distinct American Indian cultures in the deserts, mountains, and canyons of what is now Arizona. One of these groups used to be called *Anasazi*, which is a Navajo word meaning "enemies of our ancestors." Today, they are called Ancestral Puebloan people. They lived in what is now northeastern Arizona and northwestern New Mexico.

The Ancestral Puebloan people are the ancestors of the Zuni and Hopi people of Arizona and of the Pueblo people living in New Mexico. They built villages in

Montezuma Castle National Monument, near Camp Verde, was built by the Sinagua people.

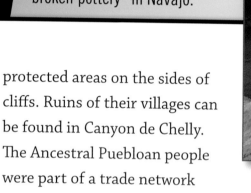

KEET SEEL
Created by the Ancestral Puebloan people, Keet Seel (also spelled Kiet Siel) is one of three well-preserved cliff dwellings that make up the Navajo National Monument in northern Arizona. The name means "broken pottery" in Navajo.

protected areas on the sides of cliffs. Ruins of their villages can be found in Canyon de Chelly. The Ancestral Puebloan people were part of a trade network that carried feathers, shells, salt, and turquoise to the peoples of the Southwest, Mexico, the Great Plains, and the Pacific Coast.

Another group of early American Indians, the Hohokam people, lived in the southern part of present-day Arizona by the Gila and Salt rivers. The Hohokams were expert farmers and grew many crops, including cotton, corn, and bean varieties. They built a large system of irrigation canals to bring water from the rivers to their fields. These canals have been discovered under the cities of Tucson and Phoenix.

The Hohokams built Casa Grande, a four-story structure between Phoenix and Tucson. The ruins of this building can be viewed at Casa Grande Ruins National Monument. Another group, the Sinagua people, built an elaborate cliff dwelling that can be seen at Montezuma Castle National Monument.

The Mogollon people lived in the desert mountains of southern Arizona and New Mexico. They farmed on the narrow ledges and moved often.

By the 1400s, the Ancestral Puebloan, Hohokam, and Mogollon people had left their traditional homelands. The Ancestral Puebloan people moved to new regions in the late 1200s, while the Mogollon and Hohokam people moved sometime around the 1300s. Experts are not sure exactly why these native peoples left the area. Lack of rainfall may have made food scarce and life harsh, forcing them to move closer to water sources such as rivers. They may have been affected by disease. New people may have moved into the area and crowded them out. They may also have started living among the other cultures in the area.

The Navajos and the Apaches began moving into the area in about 1250 CE. They came from northern regions that include parts of present-day Canada and Alaska. At the time, the Navajos and the Apaches belonged to one group. Sometime after moving to Arizona, they separated. The Navajos settled among the mesas of northeastern Arizona. The Apaches settled in the rugged mountains farther south.

Spanish Rule

Spanish soldiers and missionaries—religious people who work to convert others to their religion—began traveling north from Mexico in the years after Spain conquered Mexico in 1521. The Spanish began to hear rumors of gold and other riches in cities farther north.

In 1540, Spanish explorer Francisco Vásquez de Coronado and a large party of men left Mexico City. They traveled north with a long line of horses, cattle, and sheep. The soldiers were looking for gold and hoping to claim territory and wealth for Spain. They crossed the area that includes present-day Arizona

Quick Facts

SEVEN CITIES OF CÍBOLA

Francisco Vásquez de Coronado headed north to search for gold because of a rumor. The Spanish had been hearing tales of a place filled with riches north of Mexico called the Seven Cities of Cíbola. Returning from what is now New Mexico, a priest named Friar Marcos de Niza said he had seen the fabled place with his own eyes. No one is sure why he confirmed the rumor. Coronado was furious when he reached the area in 1541, finding only a modest village.

Coronado and his men were not successful in finding gold in the region. The region's hot, dry conditions were also challenging.

and New Mexico and headed eastward into the Great Plains. The Spanish were disappointed. They did not find gold in the dry land and sometimes fought with the native people.

In the decades after Coronado's exploration, most Europeans lost interest in the region that is now Arizona. Without the possibility of gold, they were not interested in settling an area where water could be scarce and the heat could be scorching. The area did hold interest for missionaries hoping to convert American Indian groups to Christianity, however. Around 1629, Spanish soldiers supervised the building of missions all over Arizona and New Mexico. The missionaries forced the Indians to learn Spanish culture and practice Christianity instead of their own religion. In 1680, the Pueblo people in New Mexico rebelled and drove them out.

Missionaries were more successful in southern Arizona. In 1687, a priest named Eusebio Francisco Kino visited the Tohono O'odham (Papago) and Akimel O'odham (Pima) settlements in the Sonoran Desert. In addition to telling the native people about Christianity, he taught them European-style farming. He introduced wheat and grapes and brought sheep, horses, mules, and cattle. The people began to keep livestock. Father Kino was known for treating the American Indians with kindness and respect. He eventually helped establish at least twenty-four missions in southern Arizona and northern Mexico.

Europeans were once again drawn to Arizona when a miner from the Yaqui tribe found chunks of silver near a farm called Arissona near present-day Nogales. Spaniards rushed from Mexico to dig up the ground and found more silver, but it soon ran out. Problems grew between the American Indians and the Europeans because the missionaries who followed Kino did not treat the Indians as respectfully as he had.

A statue of Eusebio Francisco Kino stands in the Wesley Bolin Memorial Plaza in Phoenix.

In 1751, the Akimel O'odhams revolted. They killed miners, settlers, and missionaries and burned their houses and churches. To protect themselves from more attacks, the Spanish built a walled presidio, or fort, at Tubac in 1752. Soldiers stayed in the presidio and a town grew outside the adobe walls. In 1775, the Spanish government established a site for a new presidio at Tucson.

Mexican Rule

Just as Americans fought the American Revolution (1775–1783) to be free of British rule, people in Mexico wanted independence from Spain. Mexico began its struggle for independence in 1810. After eleven years of war, Mexico became an independent country in 1821. Present-day Arizona was now part of Mexico instead of Spain. After the war, there was little money left to help the settlers in the Arizona area. Instead, the Mexican government gave land grants in

MAP SHOWING THE
**TERRITORY ACQUIRED
FROM MEXICO**

A large part of the Southwest was transferred to the United States after the Mexican-American War.

present-day Arizona to reward soldiers and leaders. Most of the land was used for cattle ranches. Some Spanish and Mexican land grants stayed with Arizona families for generations.

From 1846 to 1848, Mexico and the United States fought each other in the Mexican-American War. The Treaty of Guadalupe Hidalgo, signed on February 2, 1848, ended the war. Under the treaty, a huge area of the Southwest was transferred from Mexico to the United States. This land included all of today's Arizona north of the Gila River and present-day California, Nevada, and Utah. Parts of what is now New Mexico, Colorado, Wyoming, Oklahoma, and Kansas were also included. However, the towns of Tucson and Tubac were still in Mexico.

The United States wanted more land from Mexico to build a southern-route railroad to California. In 1853, Mexico agreed, in what is known as the Gadsden Purchase, to sell to the United States a strip of land south of the Gila River in present-day southern Arizona and southwestern New Mexico. The treaty providing for this purchase was ratified by the U.S. Senate the following year. Today's southern border of Arizona was set.

In the United States

Beginning in the late 1840s, Americans crossed Arizona on their way to the gold rush in California. Ferries at Yuma took them across the Colorado River. Others stayed in Arizona to search for silver and gold or to raise cattle and grow wheat.

For a number of years, present-day Arizona remained part of the Territory of New Mexico, established by the U.S. government after the Mexican-American War. In 1863, during the Civil War (1861–1865), President Abraham Lincoln signed the bill that created the separate Territory of Arizona. The new Arizona territorial government met at Prescott, the new capital. John Goodwin was the first governor of the territory.

Tensions between white people and Indians in the region increased. For years the Navajos and Apaches had fought against the Spanish and Mexicans. At first, the native peoples welcomed the American government and settlers. But misunderstandings and disagreements developed.

In an attempt to end the hostilities between the native tribes and the settlers, the U.S. government established reservations in a policy to relocate the American Indians. Some native groups agreed to go to reservations. Others did all they could to resist.

Christopher "Kit" Carson, a U.S. Army colonel, was sent by the U.S. government to pursue the Navajos. He was told to gather some eight thousand Navajos and move them to Bosque Redondo, a barren camp at Fort Sumner in New Mexico. When the Navajo people resisted, Carson and his troops burned their crops and killed their livestock. Without food, the Navajos had no choice but to surrender.

In 1864, Carson forced the Navajos to travel to Bosque Redondo on what is called the Long Walk. During this winter trek of 300 miles (480 km) and at the camp itself, thousands of Navajos died due to the harsh conditions. Those who survived the journey and did not die from smallpox or starvation at the camp were allowed to return to a reservation in Arizona after more than four years.

The Apaches, who roamed a large area covering southern Arizona, New Mexico, and northern Mexico, also had conflicts with the U.S. government. After the Civil War ended in 1865, American troops were able to concentrate on overpowering the Apache people in Arizona. Apache groups led by Cochise and Geronimo seemed impossible to catch. They knew their way in the mountains and often went to Mexico to escape the American troops.

Although Apache leader Cochise never lost a battle, he grew tired of fighting. He surrendered in 1871, later escaping when he realized the U.S. government planned to move his people to a reservation in New Mexico. He eventually agreed to go to a reservation in Arizona. Geronimo also moved to the reservation, but he and his followers left several times because of bad conditions. During his last escape, he and a small group of Apaches managed to avoid capture by the five thousand American troops pursuing them. This pursuit lasted for about a year. In 1886, however, Geronimo surrendered, ending the conflicts known as the Apache Wars.

Progress to Statehood

Despite these tensions, Arizona continued to grow and prosper. News of any silver or gold discoveries spread quickly. Young men began to move west, seeking their fortunes in the mining camps and towns. Miners

Geronimo's surrender ended the Apache Wars.

collected from streams, surface rocks, and shallow mines all the ore they could find. Then, they hurried to the next silver or gold strike.

Some of the early Arizona boomtowns gained a reputation for being lawless. Tombstone was one of these boomtowns. The prospector Ed Schieffelin found silver there in 1877. Tombstone grew rapidly into one of the biggest and most unruly towns of the West. One of the most famous shoot-outs in American history—the gunfight at the O.K. Corral—took place in Tombstone in 1881. Law enforcement officials, including Wyatt Earp and "Doc" Holliday, faced down a group of outlaws in a thirty-second showdown. Three men were killed in the gunfight. In 1887, an underground river flooded the silver mines. The boom came to an end.

After President Andrew Johnson signed a bill in 1866 chartering a railroad to California, two railroad lines were built across Arizona in the 1880s. The Southern Pacific Railroad brought in Chinese laborers to lay the tracks of the southern route across the desert. The first passenger train reached Tucson on March 20, 1880, and the Southern Pacific's transcontinental route was completed in 1881. Two years later, the Atlantic & Pacific Railroad completed a rail line through Flagstaff and across northern Arizona. Next, short rail lines were added to connect other places to the main routes.

The arrival of the railroads changed Arizona. This slow-moving, remote territory was now connected to the western and eastern states. Before the railroads, the state's ranches and farms were usually small. Ranchers and farmers produced enough food for themselves and

Wyatt Earp is best known for his involvement in Tombstone's gunfight at the O.K. Corral.

Arizona's farming industry grew after railroads reached the state. This Arizona family stands on its farmland in about 1890.

sold wheat and beef to the army forts and mining camps. Now, the large markets of California, the Midwest, and the East could be easily reached. Ranchers from Texas bought acres of Arizona grassland to create big cattle and sheep ranches. They loaded the animals onto trains bound for the stockyards of Kansas City.

By 1890, copper had replaced silver as Arizona's most valuable mineral resource. Tons of rich copper ore were mined in Bisbee at the Copper Queen Mine, which opened in 1877. Although mining copper ore and refining the ore to extract the copper were expensive, there was a new need to fill. American cities and factories needed copper for electrical wires and machinery. The railroads made it possible to send copper ore from Arizona to the nation's industrial centers.

Because Arizona was a territory, residents could not vote for the U.S. president. They had no voting representatives in Congress, but Congress could declare any territorial law invalid. The people of Arizona wanted their territory to become a state. Congress gave permission in 1910 for Arizona to write a state constitution. Congress and President William Howard Taft accepted the constitution, and Arizona became a state on February 14, 1912.

World Wars and Economic Depression

In 1917, the United States entered World War I (1914–1918). Many Arizonans joined the armed forces. Others stayed in the state, helping to produce the food and supplies that the troops needed.

Tensions grew between the owners of the copper mines in Bisbee and the miners. Miners worked under dangerous conditions for low pay. They began trying to organize and to demand better pay and working conditions. When mine owners refused their demands, a large number of Bisbee's miners went on strike. On July 12, 1917, the owners directed a large group of men to round up the miners. Any miner not willing to quit the strike was shipped on a filthy train to a remote location in New Mexico, where they were abandoned. In all, more than one thousand people were transported across the state line. The mining companies used guards to keep these people from returning. Many Americans were unhappy with the treatment of the miners and condemned the mine owners.

Beginning in 1929, hard times hit Arizona, along with the rest of the country. During the Great Depression, which continued through the 1930s, there was widespread unemployment and hardship. Eventually, Arizona began to redevelop its economy. Irrigation projects allowed agriculture to expand. The state benefited from the building of dams and highways and the resulting creation of jobs. Tourism grew, too. Word of the Grand Canyon's beauty had spread, and people wanted to see it for themselves. Arizona was also promoted as a healthful place to take a vacation or spend the winter. Health seekers came to the state, hoping that the dry climate would ease breathing problems and lung diseases such as asthma and tuberculosis.

POSTON MEMORIAL

The United States entered World War II after Japan attacked the Pearl Harbor naval base in Hawaii on December 7, 1941. In 1942, President Franklin D. Roosevelt signed an executive order requiring West Coast residents of Japanese descent to move to internment camps because of national security concerns. Arizona's Poston Relocation Center housed more than 18,000 Japanese-American detainees until its closing in 1945. Today, a memorial plaque there reads: "to all those men, women, and children who suffered countless hardships and indignities at the hands of a nation misguided by wartime hysteria, racial prejudice, and fear. May it serve as a constant reminder of our past."

After the United States entered World War II (1939–1945) in 1941, the U.S. military used the open spaces of Arizona to train pilots. The state's clear skies and good weather made it a natural location for military air bases. Factories produced aircraft, and the mines supplied minerals for defense companies. The military and the defense industries boosted Arizona's economy.

Growth and Balance

After the war, the military and defense industries stayed in Arizona. The late 1940s and early 1950s saw a boom in uranium mining, in part to provide nuclear material for military uses. Motorola set up an electronics plant in Phoenix in 1948. Thousands of people were moving to Arizona, and the economy was booming. Air conditioning units became widely available in the years after the war, allowing residents to live comfortably year-round. The state was a desirable place to relocate. Real estate developers built communities planned especially to appeal to retired people. Sun City, one of the world's first active retirement communities, opened west of Phoenix in 1960.

Over time, Arizona's progress and growth began to deplete its natural resources. People have long recognized the importance of water to Arizona. Agriculture, manufacturing, and large cities have put a serious strain on the water supply.

Arizona has two main sources of water. Surface water comes from rivers and the lakes formed by dams, while groundwater is pumped out from underground natural reservoirs. It has taken millions of years for the underground water to accumulate, and Arizona is taking out more groundwater than is being put in. Some places in Phoenix removed so much groundwater that big cracks opened in the earth.

Seven U.S. states rely on the water of the Colorado River: Arizona, California, Colorado, Nevada, New Mexico, Wyoming, and Utah. Sharing this water has been a source of conflict between the states for decades. Arizona wanted to route its share to where the need was greatest.

Sun City was one of the world's first active retirement communities. Today, it is home to almost 40,000 people.

The Central Arizona Project (CAP) is the largest aqueduct system ever built in the United States.

In 1968, President Lyndon Johnson approved construction for the Central Arizona Project (CAP). This enormous water project was designed to bring Colorado River water to central and southern Arizona. The system of aqueducts, tunnels, and pumping stations is 336 miles (541 km) long. It reaches from Lake Havasu, on the Arizona-California border, to the San Xavier Indian Reservation south of Tucson. After the U.S. Bureau of Reclamation had investigated the potential effects on the state's environment, construction began in 1973. In 1985, CAP water was first pumped to agricultural fields near Phoenix. CAP water came to Tucson in 1992.

Less groundwater is being removed from Arizona now that these systems are in place, but it is still too much. Arizonans are exploring ways to balance their water needs and water supply. This is just one example of how Arizonans continue to adjust to the changing times and find ways to help the state progress.

Important Dates

★ **10,000 BCE** Paleo-Indians live in what is now Arizona.

★ **1100s CE** Ancestral Puebloan people build complex cliff dwellings in Canyon de Chelly.

★ **1250** The Navajos and Apaches begin moving into present-day Arizona.

★ **1540s** Francisco Vásquez de Coronado's expedition explores the region.

★ **1687** Eusebio Francisco Kino begins founding missions in the area.

★ **1752** Arizona's first European settlement is established at Tubac.

★ **1821** Mexico gains independence from Spain, and present-day Arizona becomes part of Mexico.

★ **1848** The Treaty of Guadalupe Hidalgo gives most of present-day Arizona to the United States.

★ **1853** With the Gadsden Purchase, the United States buys from Mexico today's southern Arizona.

★ **1863** The U.S. government establishes the Arizona Territory.

★ **1886** Geronimo surrenders to the U.S. Army, and the Apache Wars end.

★ **1912** Arizona becomes the forty-eighth state on February 14.

★ **1922** The Colorado River Compact divides the Colorado River's water among seven states, including Arizona.

★ **1942** Japanese Americans begin living in internment camps in Arizona.

★ **1968** The Central Arizona Project, which will deliver water from the Colorado River to central and southern Arizona, is approved.

★ **1981** Arizonan Sandra Day O'Connor becomes the first female U.S. Supreme Court justice.

★ **2001** The Arizona Diamondbacks defeat the New York Yankees to win their first World Series.

★ **2008** John McCain of Arizona loses the presidential election to Barack Obama from Illinois.

★ **2011** At a political event in Tucson, Arizona congresswoman Gabrielle Giffords is shot and wounded, and six others are killed.

★ 3 ★
The People

For at least 12,000 years, people have been moving into and through what is now Arizona. They have come looking for a good place to live, to farm, and to work. The federal government takes a census, which counts all the people living in the country, every ten years. According to the 2010 Census, 6,392,017 people lived in Arizona as of April 1 of that year.

Phoenix, with a population of 1,601,587, is Arizona's largest city. It is a part of Maricopa County. The second-largest city is Tucson, in Pima County, with 548,555 people. Other large cities are Mesa, Glendale, Scottsdale, Chandler, and Tempe. Arizona also has many towns. Some of these towns have only a few thousand or a few hundred residents.

Tucson is Arizona's second-biggest city.

American Indians make up about 4 percent of Arizona's population.

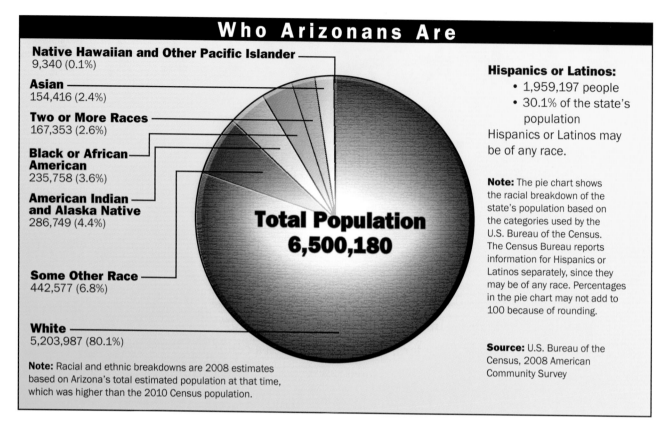

Who Arizonans Are

Native Hawaiian and Other Pacific Islander
9,340 (0.1%)

Asian
154,416 (2.4%)

Two or More Races
167,353 (2.6%)

Black or African American
235,758 (3.6%)

American Indian and Alaska Native
286,749 (4.4%)

Some Other Race
442,577 (6.8%)

White
5,203,987 (80.1%)

Total Population 6,500,180

Hispanics or Latinos:
- 1,959,197 people
- 30.1% of the state's population

Hispanics or Latinos may be of any race.

Note: The pie chart shows the racial breakdown of the state's population based on the categories used by the U.S. Bureau of the Census. The Census Bureau reports information for Hispanics or Latinos separately, since they may be of any race. Percentages in the pie chart may not add to 100 because of rounding.

Source: U.S. Bureau of the Census, 2008 American Community Survey

Note: Racial and ethnic breakdowns are 2008 estimates based on Arizona's total estimated population at that time, which was higher than the 2010 Census population.

The Faces of Arizona

Though Arizona is becoming more racially diverse, the state's population is still approximately 80 percent white. Most of Arizona's settlers were of European descent. They or their ancestors came from such countries as Spain, England, Ireland, France, Germany, or Italy.

For the most part, Arizona's racial minorities make up small percentages of the population. African Americans make up less than 4 percent of the state's people. Arizona's population is only 2.4 percent Asian American. About 4 percent of the population is American Indian.

About 30 percent of Arizona's people say they are of Hispanic or Latino origin. This means that they or their ancestors came from a Spanish-speaking nation or culture. Most Arizona Hispanics trace their roots to Mexico. Others have arrived from Guatemala, El Salvador, Colombia, Peru, and other countries in Central America, South America, and the Caribbean.

NAVAJO CODE TALKERS

Philip Johnston grew up the son of a missionary on a Navajo reservation in Flagstaff. At the beginning of World War II, Johnston met with U.S. Marine Corps officials. He suggested that military forces fighting against Japan in the Pacific use for communications a code based on the Navajo language, a code that the Japanese would not be able to crack. At the time, fewer than thirty non-Navajo people—and no Japanese—knew the Navajo language. In May 1942, the military brought in twenty-nine Navajos to develop a code system. About four hundred Navajos served as "code talkers" during the war. They used telephones and radios to transmit classified information. The code was never broken.

Albert Smith was one of the original Navajo code talkers.

American Indians

After California, Arizona is the state with the most American Indian residents. Many of these people are members of tribes that have lived in the same area for hundreds of years. Most of Arizona's American Indians live on reservations.

The Navajo Nation is located largely in the northeast corner of Arizona (and also includes land in New Mexico and Utah). It is the largest American Indian nation in the United States. It has the most members and the most land. The reservation has 180,462 residents and covers 27,673 square miles (71,673 sq km). The Tohono O'odham Nation is also large. Its land is divided into four areas in south-central Arizona. Other tribes with reservations in Arizona include the Hopi, Apache, Hualapai, Havasupai, and Yavapai people.

The tribes govern themselves. They choose their own leaders, write their own laws, and run businesses. The Ak-Chin Indian Community and the Gila River Indian Community use their land for agriculture. The Navajo and Hopi Nations mine coal.

CREATING A NAVAJO SAND PAINTING

Sand painting is a traditional art used by the Navajo people. After a healing ceremony, Navajos destroy sand paintings to symbolize the destruction of illness. Today, Navajo artists paint with sand to make lasting art. Using colored sand and crushed rock, they paint landscapes or drawings that tell a story. Much of this artwork includes images from nature, such as spiders, snakes, bears, turtles, corn, clouds, lightning, sun, and rainbows.

WHAT YOU NEED

Newspaper

Heavy paper or a smooth
   piece of plywood

Clear glue

Paintbrush

Colored sand (available
   at craft stores, or you
   can make your own)

TO MAKE COLORED SAND YOU WILL NEED

Rubber or latex gloves

3 cups (675 grams) of sand

Plastic bags

Food coloring

How to Color the Sand

Wear the gloves to protect your hands. For each color you use in your painting, put about $1/2$ cup (112 g) of sand in a plastic bag and add a few drops of food coloring. Close the bag tightly and squish the outside of the bag to work the dye into the sand. Open the bag and wait a few minutes for the sand to dry.

How to Make Your Sand Painting

Spread out a folded sheet of newspaper for each color of sand you will be using.

Draw your design on the paper or plywood. Select an area to start covering the design. Spread glue thinly with a paintbrush over this area. Take a small handful of sand and let it flow in a slow stream over the area. You can press it once with the palm of your hand and then shake off the extra sand onto a piece of newspaper. When you shake off the extra sand, try to keep the colors separate so that you can reuse the sand. Select another area and repeat until your painting is finished. Set it aside to dry—then admire your work!

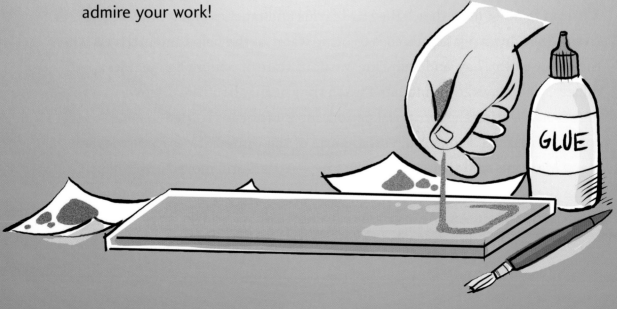

American Indian Communities and Celebrations

Many reservations in the state are open to tourists. They invite visitors to enjoy the recreation spots and areas of natural beauty. Indian tribes in the state also run gaming casinos, which fund the building of houses, schools, health clinics, and community centers. The money from these casinos also helps pay for their police and fire departments.

Many American Indians are dedicated to their communities and cultures. The Navajo Nation celebrates tradition with a seven-day festival held every year. Young people raised on Arizona's reservations blend modern American culture with traditional language and ceremonies. Many American Indian nations fund educational opportunities. The Navajo Nation has a program devoted to college scholarships and financial assistance.

Hispanic Americans

Arizona is home to nearly 2 million Hispanic Americans. The state used to be part of Mexico, and now Arizona and Mexico share a border. Spanish-speaking people have long been a large part of Arizona's culture. Spanish is widely spoken and read throughout the state. Many towns, mountains, and landmarks have Spanish names.

When the Southwest became part of the United States in 1848, many Mexican families lived there. They had farms and ranches along the Salt and Gila rivers. They dug irrigation ditches to bring water to the fields and orchards where they grew wheat, hay, and fruit. The Mexican state of Sonora had many expert miners, who moved north to mine when they heard about the discovery of gold in Arizona. During the territorial period, more Mexicans settled in what is now southern Arizona. People from other parts of the United States came too, and many Mexicans sold their land to these new settlers and moved into towns.

In the 1880s, Tucson and Tempe had a majority of Mexican-American residents. Mexican Americans were civic and business leaders. They were active in politics, and many were elected to the territorial legislature.

IMMIGRATION CONTROVERSY

U.S. Department of Homeland Security estimates say Arizona is home to about half a million undocumented immigrants—people who have entered the country without permission and documents required by the U.S. government. In the late twentieth and early twenty-first centuries, many undocumented immigrants from Mexico and, to a lesser extent, from Central America have crossed the Mexico-Arizona border. They come usually to seek better employment opportunities or to join family members. The U.S. government has increased security measures along the border in an effort to prevent undocumented immigrants from entering the country.

In April 2010, Arizona governor Jan Brewer signed a law passed by the state legislature known as SB 1070. This state law required immigrants to carry their immigration documents at all times and gave police officers the authority to detain people suspected of being undocumented until their status can be verified. Some Arizonans, troubled by undocumented immigration, supported the law. Others, concerned that it could lead to discrimination against and harassment of Hispanic Americans in Arizona, opposed it. President Barack Obama argued that SB 1070 "threatens to undermine basic notions of fairness that we cherish as Americans." The federal government began a court case to overturn the law. Governor Brewer has said, "The law is constitutional, and we'll take it all the way to the Supreme Court if necessary."

Many Hispanic Arizonans celebrate their heritage at Cinco de Mayo festivals.

In the 1900s, however, Mexican Americans often faced discrimination and other poor treatment. Children had to attend separate schools. Mexican Americans struggled to find work and to get fair wages. They joined labor unions to improve their work situation. The organization Alianza Hispano-Americana, formed in Tucson in 1894, joined forces with the NAACP (National Association for the Advancement of Colored People) in the 1950s. The groups campaigned for equal rights for citizens of Mexican descent.

In the 1960s, Mexican-American youths organized new groups throughout the Southwest. They demanded equal rights for Mexican Americans and encouraged Hispanic citizens to vote. Hispanic Americans have since regained an influential role in education, politics, and business in Arizona. The Hispanic population in Arizona is growing rapidly. According to some estimates, some day Hispanic Americans will make up a majority of the state's population.

Asian Americans

Chinese people began to arrive in Arizona in the 1850s. Like the other prospectors, they were looking for gold and silver. In the mines, they were paid low wages for dangerous work. In the towns and mining camps, they faced discrimination and abuse. In the 1870s and 1880s, railroad companies brought Chinese laborers to Arizona. These workers prepared rail beds and laid tracks for less than what white workers earned. After the mining boom ended and the railroads were completed, most Chinese left Arizona and went back to China. The few who stayed opened businesses or started farms.

Many Japanese-American families were forced to live in internment camps during World War II.

Japanese immigrants came to Arizona in the late 1890s and early 1900s. They faced injustices and unfair treatment by people who resented the competition for jobs. The Arizona legislature passed laws restricting Asian marriage partners and residency, and the U.S. Congress passed laws ending Chinese and Japanese immigration. Discrimination peaked during World War II when West Coast residents of Japanese heritage were forced to live in internment camps.

Slowly, after the war was over, the treatment of Asian Americans began to improve. In 1946, voters elected Wing F. Ong to the state's house of representatives. He was the first Chinese American to sit in any state legislature.

Today, more than 150,000 Asian Americans live in Arizona. They represent many nations, including China, Japan, India, Thailand, Cambodia, and Vietnam.

Famous Arizonans

Sharlot Hall: Writer and Historian

At age eleven, in 1881, Sharlot Hall and her family traveled from Kansas to live in the Arizona Territory. During the journey, she fell from a horse and injured her spine. She began writing to distract herself from the pain, which lasted her entire life. She collected oral histories from settlers and wrote poetry about the Southwest. From 1909 to 1912, Hall served as the territorial historian. In 1928, she began restoring the log building in Prescott that had been the territory's first capitol and governor's mansion. She died in 1943. The mansion, now called Sharlot Hall Museum, is a tribute to Arizona history.

Lewis Tewanima: Olympic Athlete

Lewis Tewanima was born on the Hopi Reservation in Second Mesa in the late 1870s. He went to the Carlisle Indian Industrial School in Pennsylvania, where his skills as a long-distance runner impressed everyone. Tewanima was a member of the U.S. Olympic teams in 1908 and 1912. In the 1912 Olympic Games, he ran in the 10,000-meter race and won the silver medal. Tewanima died in 1969 after a fall from a cliff.

Charles Mingus: Musician

Mingus was born on a military base in Nogales in 1922. He was a talented pianist and bass player. As a composer and bandleader, he reached for energetic rhythms, unexpected harmonies, and deep emotion. From the 1950s through the 1970s, Mingus played alongside other famous musicians of the era, such as Miles Davis and Duke Ellington, and recorded many groundbreaking albums. He died in 1979.

Sandra Day O'Connor: U.S. Supreme Court Justice

Sandra Day O'Connor, born in Texas in 1930, spent much of her childhood on her family cattle ranch near Duncan. O'Connor settled in Phoenix after receiving a law degree from Stanford University in California. She worked as an assistant attorney general and became an Arizona state senator in 1969. As a judge on the Maricopa County superior court and Arizona court of appeals, she earned a reputation for being hardworking and firm. O'Connor made history in 1981 when she became the first woman to serve on the U.S. Supreme Court. She retired in 2006.

Stephenie Meyer: Author

Stephenie Meyer, born in 1973, grew up in Phoenix and attended Chaparral High School in Scottsdale. After graduating from Brigham Young University in Utah, she returned to Phoenix. In 2003, Meyer had a dream about a human girl and a vampire. She turned the idea into a novel, which was published in 2005. The novel, *Twilight*, began a best-selling series of four books known as the Twilight Saga. All of the books were turned into popular movies.

Kerri Strug: Olympic Gymnast

Kerri Strug, born in 1977 in Tucson, started competing in gymnastics at the age of eight. In 1992, fourteen-year-old Strug was the youngest U.S. athlete at the Olympics. During the 1996 Olympics, Strug injured her ankle but continued to compete to help the U.S. team, dubbed the Magnificent Seven, win its first gold medal ever. For her courage, Strug received the Olympic Spirit Award.

African Americans

Many African Americans came west in the 1800s, seeking a place to live and raise a family. They built homes and ranches and worked at a variety of jobs. They prospected for gold and silver and worked for the railroads. Some African Americans were cowboys. Others started their own businesses of various kinds, such as restaurants and barbershops.

African Americans did not have an easy life in Arizona during the early 1900s. School segregation, legalized in 1909, meant that African-American children had to attend separate schools from white children. Most African Americans were restricted to living in certain neighborhoods. It was difficult for many black people to get a good education or a well-paying job. African Americans formed groups to oppose racial discrimination and unjust laws. They held demonstrations and sit-ins.

A young Arizonan eats in a local restaurant.

In 1951, the Tucson schools were desegregated, three years before the U.S. Supreme Court prohibited legally segregated schools nationwide. In 1965, the state legislature passed a civil rights act, based on the federal Civil Rights Act of 1964, intended to end discrimination against African Americans in such areas as housing, voting rights, employment, and restaurants, theaters, and other public places. African Americans began to be elected to local and state offices, and gradually life improved for them.

Arizona's Growth

Since Arizona became a state, each census has shown rapid population growth. From 2000 to 2010, Arizona's population grew by almost 25 percent. This makes Arizona the second-fastest growing state, after Nevada. Many experts expect that Arizona will continue to grow at a high rate.

Why do so many people move to Arizona? When business thrives in the state, Arizona appeals to job seekers. People are attracted by the promise of work and reasonably priced homes. They also enjoy the state's natural beauty and pleasant climate. Many people move to Arizona to be near family members. A growing number of retirees also move to Arizona to relax, play golf, or just settle into life in one of the state's many retirement communities. As the state's population continues to grow, it is clear that many people believe that Arizona has a lot to offer.

Arizona is one of the fastest-growing states in the country.

Calendar of Events

★ Yuma Lettuce Days

Yuma County is an agricultural region with a productive winter growing season. In January, the town of Yuma celebrates its status as the "Winter Lettuce Capital of the World" with local produce displays, arts and crafts, and games for kids.

★ Tucson Gem and Mineral Show

Visitors and Arizonans come to Tucson during a weekend in February to admire gems and minerals that have been collected from all over the world. A silent auction takes place on Saturday night.

★ Cactus League Baseball

During spring training in February and March, many Major League Baseball teams tune up in Arizona for the regular season. Fans attend preseason games in Tucson and Phoenix.

★ Tucson International Mariachi Conference

This conference, held every April, celebrates traditional Mexican mariachi music. Bands perform while vendors sell a variety of Mexican foods and craft items.

★ Waila Festival

Waila is a Tohono O'odham word derived from the Spanish word *baile*, which means "dance." In May, Tohono O'odham people and others gather in Tucson to enjoy waila, a partner dance blending European and Mexican music and steps.

★ July Fourth in Bisbee

The national holiday is observed in Bisbee with a traditional July Fourth parade, foot races, and fireworks. Rock-drilling contests recall Bisbee's past as a booming mining town.

★ World's Oldest Continuous Rodeo

Cowboys and cowgirls meet in Payson every year to test their roping and riding skills. One of the most popular events is the "mutton-busting" contest, in which children try to ride a sheep for at least six seconds. The rodeo has been held every August since 1884.

★ Navajo Nation Fair

The world's largest American Indian fair is held at the Navajo Nation every September. For seven days, the fair features parades, rodeos, a Miss Navajo Nation pageant, and displays of traditional Navajo artwork.

★ Arizona State Fair

More than one million people attend the state fair in Phoenix, held from mid-October to November. Visitors can check out science, farm, and animal exhibits, as well as shows and concerts and exciting rides and races.

★ El Tour de Tucson

Held on the Saturday before Thanksgiving every year, El Tour attracts cyclists of all ages and abilities. Participants may choose between races of different lengths, and all proceeds from the event are donated to local charities.

How the Government Works

A rizona has several overlapping governments: federal, state, county, city, and tribal governments. The state follows the federal, or national, laws of the U.S. government. But the state's own government also makes laws that Arizonans must follow.

The state is divided into fifteen counties. A board of supervisors chosen by popular vote leads each county. Counties are made up of cities and towns. Mayors and city councils head Arizona's cities and towns. County and city governments deal with local issues. Such issues include zoning decisions, city or town budgets, and public school matters.

Arizonans are represented in the U.S. Congress in Washington, D.C. Like all states, Arizona has two senators in the U.S. Senate. The number of members each state has in the U.S. House of Representatives is related to its population. After the 2010 Census, Arizona was entitled to nine representatives.

State Government

The state constitution went into effect when Arizona became a state in 1912. It is the basic law of Arizona. It guarantees the legal rights enjoyed by each person in the state. It describes how the state government is organized and what it does.

Like the federal government, the state government is divided into three branches: the legislative, the executive, and the judicial. Each branch has its

A statue called Winged Victory tops the Arizona Capitol Museum. The building was the state's first capitol.

Making a Living

The people of Arizona are skillful and resourceful when it comes to making a living. Many work in the traditional careers of farming, mining, or raising livestock. Many have tried new technologies and markets for their services and products.

Agriculture

Irrigation has made Arizona into an important agricultural state. Without it, much of the state's land would be too dry for faming. The state enjoys favorable weather with abundant sunshine and a nearly year-round growing season. The land of southern Arizona along the Gila River and in the west along the Colorado River is filled with huge fields of vegetables, citrus fruits, and cotton. Many leafy green crops such as lettuce do especially well in the mild winters of the low desert.

Agriculture brings in a little more than $9 billion to the state. The biggest revenue-producing crops in Arizona are lettuce, hay, and cotton. The state grows enough cotton each year to make a pair of jeans for every person in the United States.

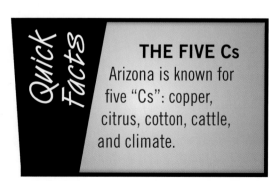

Quick Facts

THE FIVE Cs
Arizona is known for five "Cs": copper, citrus, cotton, cattle, and climate.

Farming is an important part of Arizona's economy.

The state's farms also grow broccoli, cauliflower, cantaloupe, and honeydew melons. Citrus groves produce lemons, grapefruits, oranges, and tangerines. The fruit is sold fresh or processed for frozen juice concentrate and other products. Arizona also grows carrots, potatoes, spinach, onions, parsley, and the Chinese cabbage called *bok choy*.

Arizona's lands are also used to raise livestock. Ranchers keep alive the Old West tradition of breeding cattle, sheep, and goats. Arizona's grasslands are ideal places for herds of cattle and sheep to graze. The Navajos raise Angora goats, known for their soft mohair.

A farmworker in Yuma uses an irrigation pump to send water to the fields.

RECIPE FOR CITRUS ICE CREAM

Many Arizona farms produce juicy citrus fruits such as oranges and lemons. Here is a recipe for a sweet and tangy ice cream made with these fruits.

WHAT YOU NEED

2 lemons

4 oranges

3 $\frac{1}{4}$ cups (730 g) sugar

3 cups (710 milliliters) milk

3 cups (710 ml) whipping cream

Carefully squeeze the juice from the lemons and oranges into a large mixing bowl. Be sure to strain out any pulp or seeds that might be mixed in.

Add the sugar to the lemon and orange juice. Stir the mixture thoroughly, making sure that all the sugar gets wet.

Add the milk and cream, stirring constantly until the mixture is combined.

Pour your mixture into a freezer-safe container, and store it in the freezer for at least four hours. When your ice cream is ready, enjoy it in a bowl or a cone.

This solar panel in a Tucson backyard powers outdoor lighting.

Minerals and Other Resources

Arizona's ancient volcanoes have left the land rich with valuable minerals. Lush forests that once grew years ago when the climate was wetter have been transformed into coal beds and pockets of oil and natural gas.

Arizona's first industry—mining—is still important to the state. Today's miners collect copper, molybdenum, silver, gemstones, and sand and gravel from the earth. Deep underground tunnels reach the buried deposits. When the minerals lie near the surface, a mining company simply digs a big hole. Freeport-McMoRan Copper & Gold owns an open-pit mine, as this big hole is called, north of Morenci. The mine is Morenci's biggest employer and the largest copper-producing site in North America. Copper ore is the most plentiful and valuable mineral found in Arizona. Molybdenum and silver are collected as a byproduct when copper ores are refined. Copper has many uses, especially in electronics. Molybdenum is used as a lubricant and in steel alloys.

Arizona has other natural resources above the ground. The high mountains of eastern Arizona support many acres of pine forests. These forests are harvested for timber. Arizona's waterways are also an important resource. Dams across the state store about a four-year supply of water. Hydroelectric plants built alongside the dams generate electricity for Arizonans.

Solar energy use is becoming more common in Arizona, as more people turn to renewable energy sources. In addition to helping the environment, this movement toward renewable energy is helping the state's economy by creating new jobs. Six renewable energy companies moved to Phoenix in 2010, including Power-One Inc., the largest U.S. manufacturer of renewable energy conversion devices. Among other products, Power-One creates devices that produce electricity using solar panels.

The open-pit mine north of Morenci is the largest copper-producing site in North America.

Workers & Industries

Industry	Number of People Working in That Industry	Percentage of All Workers Who Are Working in That Industry
Education and health care	581,277	19.7%
Wholesale and retail businesses	449,475	15.2%
Publishing, media, entertainment, hotels, and restaurants	366,795	12.4%
Professionals, scientists, and managers	319,127	10.8%
Construction	284,822	9.7%
Banking and finance, insurance, and real estate	235,899	8.0%
Manufacturing	219,360	7.4%
Government	157,971	5.4%
Other services	147,977	5.0%
Transportation and public utilities	146,985	5.0%
Farming, fishing, forestry, and mining	38,222	1.3%
Totals	2,947,910	100%

Notes: Figures above do not include people in the armed forces. "Professionals" includes people such as doctors and lawyers. Percentages may not add to 100 because of rounding.

Source: U.S. Bureau of the Census, 2008 estimates

Manufacturing

Arizona is a center for research and manufacturing of semiconductors. These electronic components are essential to computers, communications networks, and many electronic devices. The Intel Corporation, the world's largest semiconductor chip maker, has a large office complex in Chandler. The company employs nearly 10,000 Arizonans.

The plastics industry in Arizona is growing to meet the demand for plastic products. Manufacturers use molds to shape plastic into lightweight, strong cases for cell phones, pagers, laptop and desktop computers, electronic organizers, and other electronic devices. Arizona's plastics industry also makes disposable medical supplies and produces parts and coatings for airplanes and missiles.

The aerospace industry came to Arizona during World War II. Aircraft companies today make engines and controls for military, commercial, and private jets. They also develop missile systems for the military.

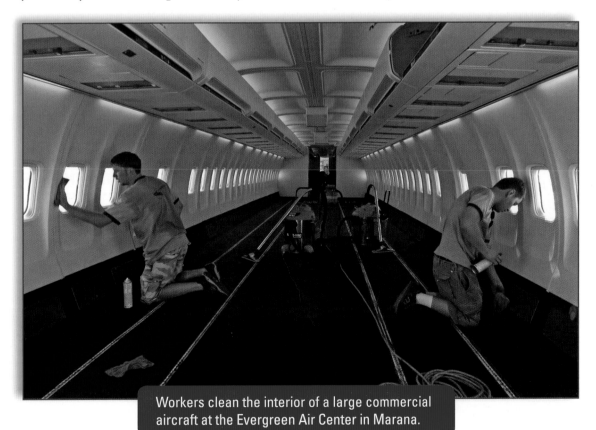

Workers clean the interior of a large commercial aircraft at the Evergreen Air Center in Marana.

Lemons

Spanish missionaries planted lemons in Arizona. Growers now produce a variety of lemons in sunny, irrigated groves. Most of the state's lemons are grown in Yuma County. Lemons from Arizona are sold throughout the world.

Construction

Construction workers build new neighborhoods for the many people moving to Arizona. They build houses, schools, stores, industrial parks, civic centers, and stadiums. Arizona's construction industry has slowed in recent years as the number of new homes being built has decreased. Many Arizonans are still employed by the industry, however.

Semiconductors

Several companies that manufacture semiconductors are located in Arizona. Semiconductors can conduct electricity at high temperatures. They are used in computers, video games, wireless phones, and many other electronics products.

Copper

Arizona produces more copper than any other state in the United States. The Morenci Mine in southeastern Arizona is the largest copper mine in the country. It produces more than 800 million pounds (360 million kilograms) of copper per year. Arizona copper is used in electrical wiring, jewelry, and all kinds of appliances and electronics products.

Tourism

Visitors come to Arizona to enjoy its natural beauty and to learn about American Indian cultures. Especially in the winter months, visitors go to Arizona resorts to relax and play golf. The lakes attract people who like to boat and fish.

Aerospace

Aerospace companies in Arizona design and build jet airplanes and missiles. They also supply many of the parts that go into aircraft. Some companies build the "black boxes" that record the details of an airplane's flight.

Science and Technology

Astronomers come to Arizona to study the Sun, the stars, and the planets. The dry air and the elevation are ideal for observing objects in space. Some telescopes use mirrors and lenses to collect visible light. Other telescopes detect radio signals and microwaves.

Several telescopes make up the Kitt Peak National Observatory in the mountains west of Tucson. The Smithsonian Institution operates the Fred Lawrence Whipple Observatory on Mount Hopkins, south of Tucson. Another collection of telescopes is stationed at the Mount Graham International Observatory, near Safford. The U.S. Naval Observatory in the mountains of Flagstaff uses instruments and measurements to provide the official time for the U.S. Department of Defense. The Lowell Observatory, also at Flagstaff, is one of the oldest observatories in the country. Established in 1894, it was named a National Historic Landmark in 1965.

Arizona is known for its biotechnology, or biotech, industry. Biotechnology uses the molecular ingredients of living things to develop new products, such as medicines. Biotechnology brings together the skills and knowledge of many scientific specialists. Today, Arizona is home to more than seventy biotech companies, located mostly in the southern part of the state.

The Kitt Peak National Observatory is home to twenty-six telescopes.

Transportation and Trade

Arizona is a transportation hub. Highways cross the state and domestic and international flights land at the airports in Phoenix, Tucson, and Yuma.

Arizona is located at a crossroads between the United States and Mexico. Long before the arrival of Europeans, the people living in Arizona carried on trade with the people living to the south in Mexico. In modern times, the Arizona-Mexico Commission (AMC) was established in 1959. This nonprofit group works to improve trade relations and help with issues relating to the shared border. Since the North American Free Trade Agreement (NAFTA), which went into effect in 1994, removed barriers to trade between the United States, Mexico, and Canada, Arizona's foreign trade activity has increased. Many of the goods traveling between Mexico and the United States pass through Tucson.

Services

Everyone needs to buy groceries, clothes, and personal items. It is not surprising, then, that food markets and retail stores are among Arizona's largest employers.

Tourism is another important part of the service industry. The tourism industry includes airports, restaurants, hotels and resorts, companies that provide organized tours, and companies that rent cars and boats.

Arizona has a wide range of natural, historical, and recreational sites. Visitors enjoy outdoor activities such as bicycling, hiking, hunting, fishing, and boating. They search for unusual landforms and look for archaeological sites and reminders of the Old West.

Professional sports are another big part of Arizona's tourism industry. Major League Baseball fans can root for the Arizona Diamondbacks. During football season, fans cheer on the National Football League's Arizona Cardinals. The state is also home to two professional basketball teams: the Phoenix Suns of the National Basketball Association and the Phoenix Mercury of the Women's National Basketball Association. Despite its climate, Arizona even has a team in the National Hockey League—the Phoenix Coyotes.

Many people in Arizona work in jobs that serve their community. They work in city, county, or state government. Many Arizonans find jobs at the state's colleges and universities, including Arizona State University, Northern Arizona University, and the University of Arizona. Some Arizonans work as police officers or park rangers.

The U.S. military is a major employer in Arizona. The Air Force, Army, and Marine Corps have bases in Arizona where pilots and soldiers are stationed and train. The activities at the bases are supported by many civilian, or nonmilitary, employees and suppliers.

Arizona relies on its growing industries and its hardworking residents. Working together and adjusting to today's economic challenges, Arizonans continue to strive to make their state successful.

Many tourists come to Arizona to enjoy outdoor activities.

State Flag & Seal

The colors of the flag of Arizona recall the history of the state. The red and yellow rays in the upper half of the flag represent the red and yellow flags carried by Spanish explorers. The blue of its lower half matches the blue of the U.S. flag. The copper-colored star in the middle commemorates Arizona as the largest producer of copper in the nation. Thirteen red and yellow rays represent the thirteen original colonies of the United States and are designed to mimic a setting sun. The flag, designed by Colonel Charles W. Harris, was adopted in 1917.

Arizona's state seal is in the shape of a shield. It shows the sun rising between the mountains. On the right side, there is a dam, a reservoir, irrigated fields, and cattle. To the left, a miner stands in front of a quartz mill. The motto at the top, Ditat Deus, means "God enriches" in Latin. A circular band bearing the words "Great Seal of the State of Arizona" surrounds the seal. Printed along the bottom is the year that Arizona became a state—1912.

ARIZONA

Map legend:

- Interstate Highways
- U.S. Highways
- City or Town
- State Capital
- Indian Reservation
- National Monument
- National Forest
- National Park
- National Recreation Area
- Highest Point in the State
- Only point in the U.S. common to four state corners

miles
0   20

Labels on map:

15 · Kaibab Reservation · Page · Lake Powell · 163 · Kayenta · 160
Grand Canyon National Park · ALT 89 · 89 · Tuba City · Navajo Nation · 160 · 191
Grand Canyon National Park · Colorado River · Grand Canyon · Kaibab National Forest · Little Colorado River · Hopi Reservation · Ganado · Canyon de Chelly National Monument
Lake Mead · Lake Mead National Recreation Area · Havasupai Reservation · Hualapai Reservation · Colorado River
Lake Mohave · 93 · Kingman · Bullhead City · Kaibab National Forest · HUMPHREYS PEAK · Flagstaff · 40 · 191
Fort Mojave Reservation · 40 · Big Sandy River · Prescott National Forest · Verde River · Sedona · Winslow · Coconino National Forest · Zuni Reservation
Lake Havasu City · Lake Havasu · Alamo Lake · 93 · Santa Maria River · Prescott · Apache-Sitgreaves National Forest
Parker · Bill Williams River · Colorado River Tribes · 60 · 17 · Tonto National Forest · Payson · Horseshoe Reservoir · Fort Apache Reservation · Eagar · 60 · Apache-Sitgreaves National Forest
Colorado River · 10 · 60 · Salt River Reservation · Bartlett Reservoir · Theodore Roosevelt Lake · Salt River · Black River · San Carlos Apache Reservation · 191
Glendale · Phoenix · Scottsdale · Tonto National Forest · 60 · Globe · 70
95 · Tempe · Gila River Reservation · 60 · San Carlos Lake · Gila River · Safford
Gila River · Ak-Chin Community · 10 · Florence · San Pedro River · Coronado National Forest · 191
Yuma · 8 · Tornillo Wash · 8 · Casa Grande · Brawley Wash · 10 · San Simon River · 10
Ajo · Organ Pipe Cactus National Monument · Tohono O'odham Nation · San Xavier Reservation · Tucson · Coronado National Forest
19 · Coronado National Forest · Bisbee · Coronado National Forest · 191

N · W · E · S

Arizona March Song

words by Margaret Rowe Clifford
music by Maurice Blumenthal

BOOKS

Aldridge, Rebecca. *The Hoover Dam*. New York: Chelsea House, 2009.

Augustin, Byron. *The Grand Canyon*. New York: Benchmark, 2009.

Dyan, Penelope. *One Big Hole in the Ground, A Kid's Guide to Grand Canyon, USA*. Jamul, CA: Bellissima Publishing, 2010.

Ponte, June. *Fun and Simple Southwestern State Crafts: Colorado, Oklahoma, Texas, New Mexico, and Arizona*. Berkeley Heights, NJ: Enslow Publishers, 2009.

WEBSITES

Arizona State Historical Society:
http://www.arizonahistoricalsociety.org

Official Arizona State Website:
http://az.gov

Sharlot Hall Museum:
http://sharlot.org

State of Arizona Kids' Page:
http://www.azlibrary.gov/links/kidsAZ.aspx

Visit Arizona:
http://www.arizonaguide.com

Kathleen Derzipilski is a research editor who specializes in children's nonfiction. She lives in San Diego, California.

Amanda Hudson is a children's book editor and writer. She lives outside of New York City, but loves visiting her brother and his wife in Phoenix—especially in March.

Page numbers in **boldface** are illustrations.